The Little Book of Toasts

THE LITTLE BOOK OF TOASTS

A HAPPY COLLECTION FOR ALL OCCASIONS

Compiled and Edited by Barbara Kunz Loots
Illustrated by Peter Lippmann

Hallmark Editions

Copyright © 1975 by Hallmark Cards, Inc., Kansas City, Missouri.
All Rights Reserved. Printed in the United States of America.
Library of Congress Catalog Card Number: 74-20498. Standard Book Number: 87529-433-2.

Here's to the best of us,
Here's to the rest of us,
Here's to our friendships,
    old ones and new!
Here's joy and wealth to you,
Peace and good health to you,
Here's to a good life —
    for all and for you!

THE ART OF TOASTING

I drink to the general joy of the whole table.
Shakespeare

This generous toast, one of many in Shakespeare's plays, can be quoted on nearly any occasion when a toast is called for. The art of toasting itself is much older than Shakespeare, however. In one form or another, the custom probably dates back as far as men and women have gathered together to enjoy good food, good drink and congenial company.

The word "toast" as we use it seems to have originated in an old European custom. A piece of toast dropped into each cup of wine quickly sank to the bottom. Then the host spoke a few appropriate words and challenged guests to drain their cups "to the toast." Perhaps repetition of the challenge on important occasions accounts for the considerable merriment at some of ye olde feastes! Nowadays, a sip is considered sufficient after each toast, and the glasses lifted are filled, not always with wine, but with almost any beverage from martinis to milk.

Today, the custom of the toast is enjoyed on both formal and informal occasions. And these gracious, often witty, tributes — to the host and hostess, to the occasion, and to the company — are as welcome as friendship itself.

Here is a bright collection of new and traditional toasts. Keep a few favorites in mind. Revise them to suit your audience and your imagination. Then, whenever the occasion arises for you to rise to the occasion — Here's to it! And most of all…HERE'S TO YOU!

AS THEY SAY IN...

American	Down the hatch!
French	A votre santé!
Italian	Salute!
Spanish	Salud!
German	Prosit!
Hebrew	L'chayim!
Polish	Vivat!
Russian	Za vashe zdorovye!

A TOAST TO THE HOST AND OTHER FRIENDS

Here's to your good health, and your family's good health,
and may you all live long and prosper.
>   *Washington Irving*

>   A toast to every one of you,
>   No matter where you're from;
>   May the best day in your life so far
>   Be worse than your worst to come.

Here's to prosperity…but in the words of Mark Twain,
"When you ascend the hill of prosperity,
may you not meet a friend coming down."

❦

Here's to us that are here, to you that are there,
and the rest of us everywhere.
Kipling

❦

Here's to beauty, wit, and the fruit of the vine…
to a full stomach, a heavy pocketbook and a light heart.

❦

Here's to the fellowship
in every sip of friendship's brew!

Friendship is the wine of life.
Let us drink of it and to it!

Here's to the sum of happiness:
something to do, something to love,
and something to hope for.

To the Host and Hostess:
An ancient proverb says,
"The heart that gives gathers."
May you always gather
as generously as you give!

To our health, which gives us hope —
and to hope, which gives us everything!

TOASTS WITH A TOUCH OF WIT

Here's to the happiest hours of my life,
spent in the arms of another man's wife:
My Mother!

May you be in Heaven half an hour
before the devil knows you're dead.

Here's to woman! Would that we could fall into
her arms without falling into her hands.
Ambrose Bierce

To us — may we always do right; this will gratify some people and astonish the rest.

I drink to your health when I'm with you,
I drink to your health alone,
I drink to your health so often
I'm worried about my own.

Here's to a clear conscience —
or a poor memory.

FOR BIRTHDAYS

Here's to life — a little gleam of time
between two eternities.

◎

Here's to the world, the merry old world,
To its days both bright and blue;
Here's to the future, be it what it may,
And here's to the best — that's you!

◎

There is no cure for birth and death —
  let us enjoy the interval.
                    George Santayana

A toast to the day
        That's especially for you:
May your pleasures be many,
    Your troubles be few!
May the day bring you hours
    of enjoyment
      and then
May its joys be repeated
    Again and again!

☙

Here's to birthdays!
As John Adams tells us,
an ass is older at thirty
than a man is at eighty years.

The good die young —
here's hoping
you'll live to a ripe old age!

Here's to maturity!
When there's snow on the roof,
there's fire in the furnace!

☯

To the old, long life and treasure;
To the young, all health and pleasure.
Ben Jonson

☯

Here's to old age.
You can take a nap
when you feel like it
without being called lazy.

ON THE OCCASION OF MARRIAGE

To the lovely bride:
May your joys be as many as
the petals of your bouquet.

From the Parents
It is written:
"When children find true love,
parents find true joy!"
Here's to your joy and ours,
from this day forward!

The Bride's Toast:
I drink to myself and one other,
And may that one other be he
Who drinks to himself and one other,
And may that one other be me.

☙

Here's to your wedding day:
the beginning of a beautiful forever!

☙

A toast to:
something old, something new,
something borrowed, something blue,
love to share and dreams come true,
and all life's joys for both of you!

To the bride and groom —
May your love be as endless
as your wedding rings!

A toast to love and laughter
and happily-ever-after!

The Groom's Toast:
Here's to my wife,
my bride and joy!

To the father of the bride…
   who gives his lovely daughter away
      to a man who isn't nearly good enough for her…
so he can have grandchildren
   brighter and better than anyone else's!

FOR A WEDDING ANNIVERSARY

Here's to the bonds of love
uniting husband and wife —
Long, yet too short,
   they spend a happy life.

◎

An anniversary toast
to precious moments present,
to precious moments past,
to precious moments yet to come
and to a love that will always last.

Here's to you both —
a beautiful pair,
on the birthday
of your love affair!

Here's to the past —
And the joys you have known,
Here's to the present —
This day all your own,
And here's to the future —
May every new day
Be especially happy
For you, every way!

SILVER ANNIVERSARY

Today…
may the joys you've shared
through twenty-five years
shine like silver souvenirs.

Twenty-five silver years
   since you exchanged vows
   and your new life began…
Twenty-five silver years
   of growing and loving
   and living as one…
May the next twenty-five be golden!

☙

May your silver anniversary
   be rich in memory,
May the future years be golden
   with opportunity
For you deserve to have your dreams
   become reality.

GOLDEN ANNIVERSARY

Here's to both of you with cheers
   For your fifty golden years!

☙

  Tennyson said,
"Love is the only gold."
 So here's to you, and to your love
through fifty golden years.

FOR BUSINESS OCCASIONS

SPECIAL ACCOMPLISHMENTS

It is said,
"An honor won is a promise of more."
Here's to your fine accomplishment.
May it lead to even greater success for you.

☙

Congratulations on your promotion!
Here's to a world of good luck,
a world of success,
a world of happiness!

Here's to a wonderful beginning
and never-ending success!

ANNIVERSARY

Here's to you on your anniversary —
May success and happiness be
   yours in everything you do!

A very special day like this
Calls for a special toast —
So here's to future days that bring
The things you want the most,
Here's to success and happiness
In everything you do,
As year by year your hopes and plans
Work out just right for you.

RETIREMENT

Think of us once in awhile
For we'll be thinking of you
And wishing you the best of luck
In all you've planned to do!

Congratulations
And best wishes,
Now your time is all your own —
May these years
Be the happiest years
That you have ever known.

HOLIDAYS

THE FOURTH OF JULY AND OTHER PATRIOTIC OCCASIONS

Let us, as did the founding fathers, mutually pledge to each other our lives, our fortunes, and our sacred honor!

◎

> To our candidate, (name).
> May our great men be good,
> and our good men, great!

Here's to the United States of America. Let freedom ring!

CHRISTMAS

May you have
   the gladness of Christmas
     which is hope…
The spirit of Christmas
     which is peace…
The heart of Christmas
     which is love.

◉

Here's to us all —
God bless us every one.
Dickens

Here's to the ones that deserve them:
Good health, good luck, good cheer,
A more-than-merry Christmas
And a better-than-ever year!

MERRY CHRISTMAS

German	Froeliche Weihnachten
French	Joyeux Noel
Spanish	Feliz Navidad
Italian	Buone Natale
Hawaiian	Mele Kalikimaka
Swedish	Glad Yul

Joy to the world — and especially to you!

THE NEW YEAR

Let us enjoy the coming year —
it is the youngest age we have left.

To your health,
happiness and prosperity
all through the new year!

❦

Ring out the old, ring in the new,
Ring, happy bells, across the snow:
The year is going, let him go;
Ring out the false, ring in the true.
Tennyson

❦

Here's to yesterday's memories,
today's joys and
tomorrow's dreams!

ST. PATRICK'S DAY

May the saints protect you,
And sorrow neglect you,
And bad luck to the one
That doesn't respect you!

THANKSGIVING

Here's to the blessings of the year,
Here's to the friends we hold so dear,
To peace on earth, both far and near!

FOR OTHER SPECIAL OCCASIONS... AND SPECIAL PEOPLE

TO YOUR NEW HOME

Here's to your new home!
Every time you walk in the door,
Hope you'll enjoy it more and more!

To your new home…
   a wonderful beginning
   to wonderful memories.

TO FATHER

Here's to you, Father,
with memories of happy times —
times you made happen!

☻

Here's to the very best of dads —
the very best of days!

TO MOTHER

To the sweetest mother
there ever was,
for everything she is and does!

Here's to you, Mother —
For warm memories of yesterday,
For happiness today,
For the promise of tomorrow.

FOR THE NEW BABY

The happiness that fills your hearts
Is shared by others, too,
Here's to the very best in life
For your baby and for you!

BON VOYAGE

Here's to a wonderful time,
Don't do anything we wouldn't do!

Here's to a wonderful time
   aboard ship,
Adventures ashore,
And a good return trip!

Here's to a wonderful vacation!
Hope you go where you like…
   and like where you go!

Live it up
on your vacation!
Live it down
when you get back!

Here's a health to all those whom we love,
And a health to all those who love us,
Here's a health to all those who love those
who love those
Who love those who love those who love us.